1 十二単　東京国立博物館
JŪNIHITOE (lady's ceremonial dress). *National Museum, Tokyo.*

Textiles

Text by

TOMOYUKI YAMANOBE

English adaptation by

LYNN KATOH

CHARLES E. TUTTLE COMPANY

RUTLAND, VERMONT & TOKYO, JAPAN

Publisher's Note

The text which follows, though adapted for Western readers and slightly changed because of space considerations, is based directly upon Mr. Yamanobe's excellent Japanese text. The careful reader will note an occasional inconsistency of style or fact between the English captions beside the plates, prepared at the time of the original Japanese edition, and the English text, especially prepared and, where necessary, corrected for this edition. We believe the reader will agree, however, that these slight inconsistencies are more than offset by the quality of the text and plates themselves.

Published by the Charles E. Tuttle Company, of Rutland, Vermont & Tokyo, Japan, by arrangement with Kodansha, Tokyo. All rights reserved by Kodansha, without whose written permission no part of the contents of this book may be reproduced.

Library of Congress Catalog Card No. 57–10686

First English edition, 1957

Printed in Japan by Dai Nippon Printing Co., Tokyo

Japanese Textiles

In today's age of industrialism the machine has gained the upper hand and man is fast losing the dignity of individual handiwork. In the field of textiles, however, Japan still retains, though no doubt with a precarious hold, a handicraft tradition of dyeing and weaving that has been handed down from the misty past. She is well-nigh unique in this regard, and yet at the same time she ranks foremost among the nations of the world in the production of modern fabrics, from the most up-to-date textile mills.

The linens of Niigata Prefecture and the silks of Ibaraki Prefecture are still woven on the most primitive of hand looms. In Kyoto and Aichi Prefectures the tie-and-dye technique called Shibori is still used just as it was generations ago; it is a laborious, time-consuming hand technique which, to the uninitiated, seems almost a kind of legerdemain. The many types of woven splash designs called Kasuri—Omeshi, Oshima, Yuki Tsumugi, Ojiya Chijimi, and the like—are so common in Japan that the Japanese scarcely notice them, and yet they have recently won high praise from the French couturiers for their great effectiveness as handmade textiles. Not only in dyeing and weaving but in designs, in color combinations, and in the very grace of the kimono lines the Japanese have much to regard with justifiable pride.

To gain an idea of the richness of this traditional handicraft a brief survey of its historical highlights may prove of interest and will also provide a background for the many examples of Japanese textile art illustrated in this book.

The beginnings. As a result of archeological research it is now generally believed that dyeing and weaving in Japan was begun after the earliest type of Stone Age pottery, known as Jomon ware, had given way to Yayoi pottery, which continued on into the age of metals. The Japanese Stone Age is considered to have lasted from the second and third centuries B.C. to the third century A.D. Fragments of what are thought to have been weaving looms have been excavated in the ruins of the Yayoi period at Karako-ike in Nara Prefecture and at Toro in Shizuoka Prefecture. These earliest looms were probably of the primitive type that can be seen today among collections of implements used by the aboriginal Ainu, who still live in small numbers in the northernmost island, Hokkaido. Further evidence of the probable beginnings of weaving in Japan is provided by the fact that the impressions on the bottom of Yayoi pottery are those of a cloth weave, whereas Jomon pottery show impressions made by baskets or matting. Judging from the number and coarseness of the threads impressed in the Yayoi pottery, the material was evidently woven from fibers of hemp, paper mulberry, or wisteria vines. This, then, is the state in which weaving stood until the first or second centuries of the Christian era.

The first documentary record concerning weaving in Japan is found in the Chinese Han chronicles of the third century, in *The History of the Three Kingdoms*. This mentions that the Japanese were then engaged in sericulture, and also records that in the years 238 and 243 a Japanese empress presented gifts of brocades called Yamato and Kosei to the king of Wei, one of the Three Kingdoms. That the material is called brocade shows that it must have been some kind of very fine fabric.

In the Japanese chronicles we find a record stating that in the year 188 the Chinese king Koman presented to the Japanese emperor Chuai a gift of silkworm eggs. Later, so the record goes, King Koman's son, Yuzu, came to Japan with twenty-five thousand subjects from 127 provinces, all of whom became naturalized Japanese subjects. Frequent note is made of many naturalized Chinese, who came by way of Korea, and of the great impetus given weaving by the new methods they brought in.

Even though the reliability of such ancient records may be held in doubt, proof of great technical developments is to be found in the iron artifacts dating from the fourth and fifth centuries. There have been found, rusted on these artifacts, remains of what, without doubt, was silk. Judging from the technique of workmanship of the iron objects, methods employed in weaving must also have attained an equally high level.

Asuka-Nara period (552–794). The earliest textiles which can be studied at first-hand are those of the Asuka-Nara period. Almost all of these have been preserved at Nara either in the Horyu-ji, the oldest temple in Japan and probably the oldest wooden building in the world, or in the Shoso-in. The Shoso-in is a veritable treasure house, for it contains not only textiles but all manner of objects stored intact since the year 756, twelve centuries ago. It is, in fact, an imperial repository housing the treasures and belongings of the emperor Shomu. Made of wood, its unique structure controls the humidity and accounts for the marvelous preservation of its contents. Nowhere in the world can a comparable collection of eighth-century fabrics be seen. The number alone is astounding. Already fifty years have been spent in the sorting, restoring, and cataloguing of these textiles, and still it will take several more decades to complete the task.

This was the period centering around Shotoku Taishi, the great sage-prince who did so much to foster learning and the arts and to introduce Buddhism into Japan. It was under his patronage that a great influx of culture flowed in directly from China and, by way of China and Korea, from India, Persia, Arabia, and even the far distant Roman Empire. This accounts for the fact that one can see in these hand-dyed and hand-woven materials of the Nara period evidence of a very advanced culture, and in the range of their design and color an extraordinary universality.

These handmade textiles were classified according to thickness or quality of thread. Aya (Plate 6) was the name for any material in which the design was woven by means of twills or plaited weaves. Nishiki (brocade) was any material with a design woven of several colors, including both Yoko Nishiki, in which the pattern was in the woof (Plate 12), and Tate Nishiki, with the pattern in the warp (Plate 4). There were also brocades in which the design was made by linked weaving, the Tsuzure of today. And the many flat-woof weaves of mottled threads were known as Kanto brocade (Plate 3).

The greatest number of these brocades are of a complicated weaving technique with such wonderful colors and designs that even today they are astonishing; particularly so is the thin silk gauze called Ra (Plate 5), a fabric of exquisite fineness. The art of weaving this was once lost but has been rediscovered, and the technique is now designated by the Japanese government as an intangible cultural asset.

Various methods of dyeing were employed. The Kokechi, today known as Shibori (Plate 11), included several tie-and-dye methods, even to a complicated one of tying and dyeing both sides. Rokechi or wax dyeing was a kind of batik, complicated designs of several colors being produced by applying wax with either stencils or brushes. Kyokechi (Plate 5) was a kind of stencil dyeing in which, before dyeing, the material was folded double and clamped between two thin boards having perforated designs; this was an exceedingly precise and exact technique, the design having a most artistic effect, but the exact details of the method are no longer known.

Considering the great skills achieved in the textiles of the Asuka-Nara period and the considerable influence they still exert on Japanese textiles today, it can well be said that this age saw the foundation and real beginning of Japanese textile art.

Heian-Kamakura period (794–1333). Dyeing and weaving in the Heian-Kamakura period gradually leveled off from the lavishness of the Nara period to a fashion more suited to the spirit of the times. The Chinese fashion of rich brocades for ceremonial robes changed for the most part to an attire of heavy layers of kimono— the Junihitoe fashion (Plate 1). This brought about a great change in the weaving industry. No longer were colorful, large-patterned designs effective for the new mode. Small, regular woven designs became the style. A glimpse of many shades of color at the neck, sleeve, and hemline was the sought-after effect, with subtle gradations of the color scheme according to the season.

Such sets of kimono called for great amounts of material. The weavers, suddenly confronted with a huge increase in demand, naturally shunned complicated and time-consuming methods. Compared with the intricate techniques employed in the preceding period, the trend even in the weaving of brocades and gauzes was toward the simpler methods. Raised weaves and double weaves were developed. Inevitably, simplification led to a deterioration of the handicraft, and by the end of the Kamakura period a coarseness of weaving and fixity of design had become very conspicuous. A

2 天寿国繡帳 飛鳥時代 奈良 中宮寺
BUDDHIST PARADISE EMBROIDERY. Asuka Period.
Chū-gū-ji Temple, Nara.

very interesting point to note at this time was the increasing popularity among the common people of a free and rather picturesque design in their clothes. This is a very definite hint of the trend which was to become the vogue in the Kosode fashion, a radical change in kimono style of the Muromachi era.

Muromachi period (1336–1568). From one point of view, the Muromachi period was a dark age for the handicrafts of dyeing and weaving. The country was always in the turmoil of war, and the people's thoughts were more occupied with obtaining daily necessities than with beautiful clothes. From another point of view, however, this selfsame feudal warfare led to the spread of culture, which had heretofore centered only around the capital, Kyoto, to fiefs from one end of the land to the other. This was a result of the vying of the daimyo in developing industries in their own particular fiefs. This age, then, can be looked upon rather as a preparatory interval for the creation of the golden age of textile art that flowered in the Kosode fashion of the Momoyama-Edo period.

One signal step was the gradual change in the shape of the kimono sleeve from the long, trailing Junihitoe fashion to the shorter type which became the distinguishing characteristic of the Kosode fashion. This change in the shape of the sleeve and, consequently, in the over-all effect of the kimono naturally led to changes in design, greatly accelerating the development of free, handpainted patterns. Since, however, the emphasis of the past several centuries had been almost exclusively on woven designs, now the only remaining non-weaving design technique was the tie-and-dye. For lack of other techniques, this was used for the first handpainted-design dyeing, resulting in the textile style known as Tsujigahana dyeing. Controlled by the exacting technique of tying and dyeing but meeting the demand for a free, handpainted design, these Tsujigahana materials (Plate 27) had a restrained elegance coupled with a certain quietness.

This age also saw the introduction of new textiles from Ming China including such as Kinran (gold brocade), Donsu (silk damask), Chirimen (a kind of crepe), and Kaiki (taffeta). Moreover, in the latter part of the period, Spanish ships brought wool fabrics and

(*continued on p. 47*)

6

3 広東錦（法隆寺裂）　飛鳥時代　東京国立博物館
KANTŌ BROCADE (fragment preserved in Hōryūji Temple).
Asuka Period. *National Museum, Tokyo.*

4 蜀江錦（法隆寺裂）　飛鳥時代　東京国立博物館
SHU-CHIANG BROCADE (fragment preserved in Hōryūji Temple).
Asuka Period. *National Museum, Tokyo.*

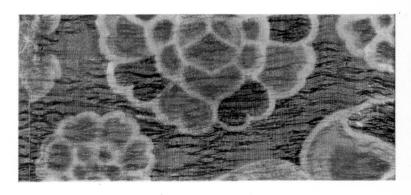

5 緑地羅花文纐纈（正倉院裂）　奈良時代　東京国立博物館
" JAMMED DYEING," SILK GAUZE (fragment preserved in Shōsōin).
Nara Period. *National Museum, Tokyo.*

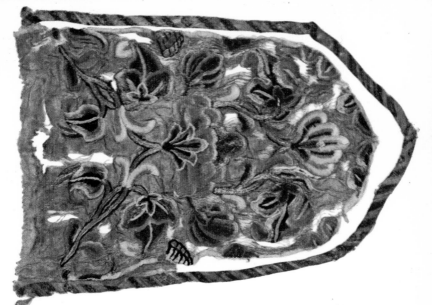

6 白地花模様刺繍裂（正倉院裂） 奈良時代 東京国立博物館
FLORAL DESIGN EMBROIDERY (fragment preserved in Shōsōin).
Nara Period. *National Museum, Tokyo.*

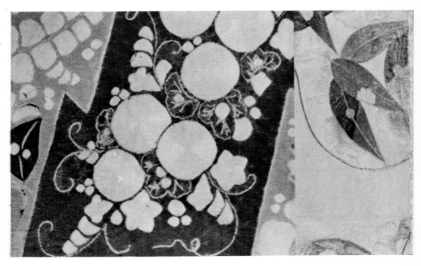

7 花卉模様辻が花裂 桃山時代 京都 瑞泉寺
TSUJIGAHANA DYEING. Momoyama Period. *Zuisenji Temple, Kyoto.*

8　納戸地南蛮船模様（能衣裳）　江戸時代　東京　前田育徳会
NOH PLAY COSTUME, NUIHAKU TYPE (embroidery and gold leaf appliqués). Early Edo Period. *Maeda Ikutokukai Collection, Tokyo.*

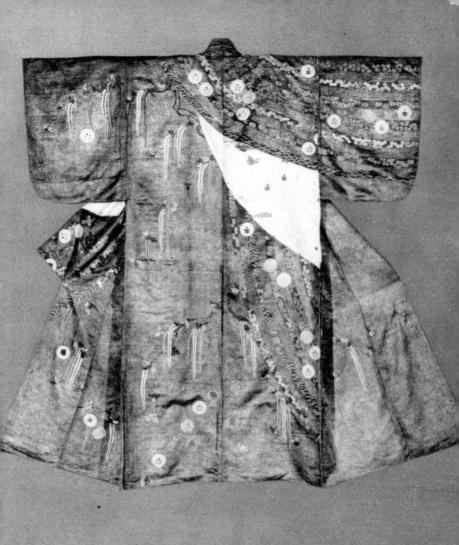

9 & 10 花卉模様縫箔小袖　江戸初期　鎌倉　岡本家
KOSODE (short sleeved kimono), NUIHAKU TYPE.
Early Edo Period. *Okamoto Collection, Kamakura.*

11 七宝模様纐纈裂（正倉院裂）　奈良時代　東京国立博物館
KŌKECHI, TIE-DYEING (fragment preserved in Shōsōin).
Nara Period. *National Museum, Tokyo.*

12 碧地花文錦（正倉院裂）　奈良時代　東京国立博物館
BROCADE, FLORAL DESIGN ON BLUE GROUND (fragment preserved
in Shōsōin). Nara Period. *National Museum, Tokyo.*

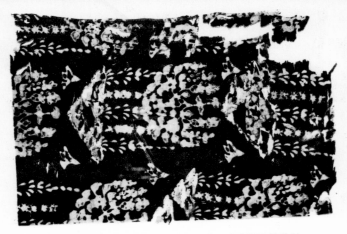

13 花鳥模様﨟纈裂（正倉院裂）　奈良時代　東京国立博物館
BATIK, FLOWER-AND-BIRD DESIGN (fragment preserved in Shōsōin).
Nara Period. *National Museum, Tokyo.*

14 水引裂　鎌倉時代　京都　教王護国寺
CURTAIN AROUND SIDES OF OPEN-AIR STAGE (detail).
Kamakura Period. *Kyō-ō-gokokuji Temple, Kyoto.*

15　纐纈色綾地纐纈裂（正倉院）　奈良時代　東京国立博物館
TIE-DYEING (fragment preserved in Shōsōin).
Nara Period. *National Museum, Tokyo.*

16　三面宝珠錦　平安時代　京都　仁和寺
BROCADE, FLAMING "SACRED GEM" DESIGN.
Heian Period. *Ninnaji Temple, Kyoto.*

17　金紅片身替厚板（能衣裳）　江戸時代　東京国立博物館
NOH PLAY COSTUME, ATSUITA TYPE.
Early Edo Period. *National Museum, Tokyo.*

20 & 21　吉原細見模様小袖　江戸後期　鎌倉　長尾美術館
KOSODE, YŪZEN-DYEING WITH DESIGN OF YOSHIWARA GAY QUARTER.
Late Edo Period. *Nagao Museum, Kamakura.*

22 & 23　短冊藤模様唐織（能衣裳）　江戸中期　東京国立博物館
NOH PLAY COSTUME, KARAORI TYPE, POETIC PANELS AND WISTERIA
DESIGN.　Middle Edo Period. *National Museum, Tokyo.*

24　黒地花卉模様小袖　桃山時代　東京国立博物館

KOSODE, TIE-DYEING AND EMBROIDERY WITH FLORAL DESIGN ON
BLACK AND BLUE GROUND. Momoyama Period. *National Museum,
Tokyo.*

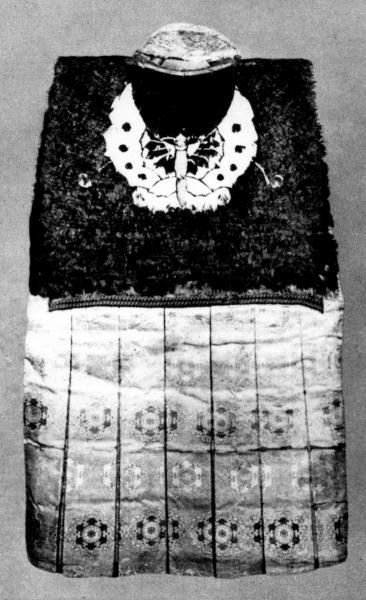

25 鳥毛陣羽織 桃山時代 東京国立博物館
JIMBAORI DECORATED WITH FEATHERS (coat worn over armour).
Momoyama Period. *National Museum, Tokyo.*

26　扇面散鉄線花片身替縫箔（能衣裳）　桃山時代　東京国立博物館
NOH PLAY COSTUME, NUIHAKU TYPE. Momoyama Period.
National Museum, Tokyo.

27 白紫地竹模様辻が花染小袖（徳川家康所用） 江戸初期
　　大彦染織美術研究所
KOSODE, TSUJIGAHANA DYEING WITH BAMBOO DESIGN.
Early Edo Period. *Daihiko Institute of Dyeing and Embroidery,
Tokyo.*

28 黒地梅模様振袖（桂昌院所用）　江戸初期　東京　護国寺
FURISODE, (long sleeved kimono), TIE-DYEING AND EMBROIDERY
WITH PLUM TREE DESIGN ON BLACK GROUND (detail).
Early Edo Period. *Gokokuji Temple, Tokyo.*

29　白地秋草模様小袖　江戸中期　尾形光琳筆
KOSODE, HAND-PAINTED DESIGN BY OGATA KŌRIN.
Middle Edo Period. *National Museum, Tokyo.*

30 & 31　風景模様小袖　江戸中期　京都　丸紅
KOSODE, YŪZEN DYEING.
Middle Edo Period.　*Marubeni Collection, Kyoto.*

32 & 33　浅葱地石畳鉄線花模様厚板唐織（能衣裳）
　　　　　江戸中期　東京国立博物館
NOH PLAY COSTUME, ATSUITA-KARAORI TYPE.
Middle Edo Period.　*National Museum, Tokyo.*

35　のし模様振袖　江戸中期　京都　友禅史会
FURISODE, YŪZEN DYEING AND EMBROIDERY WITH "NOSHI"
DESIGN. Middle Edo Period. *Yūzenshikai Collection, Kyoto.*

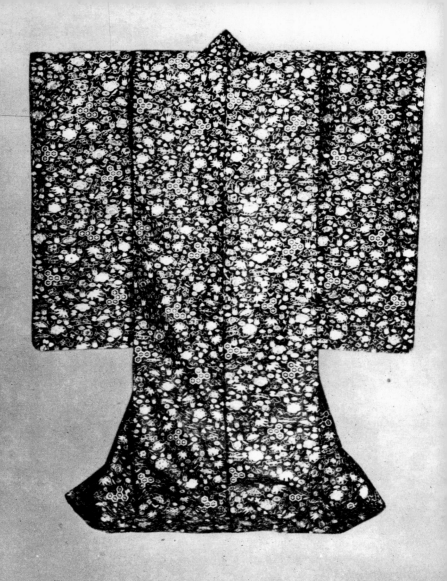

36　黒地宝尽し模様腰巻　江戸中期　東京国立博物館
KOSHIMAKI (lady's ceremonial summer gown) EMBROIDERY.
Middle Edo Period. *National Museum, Tokyo.*

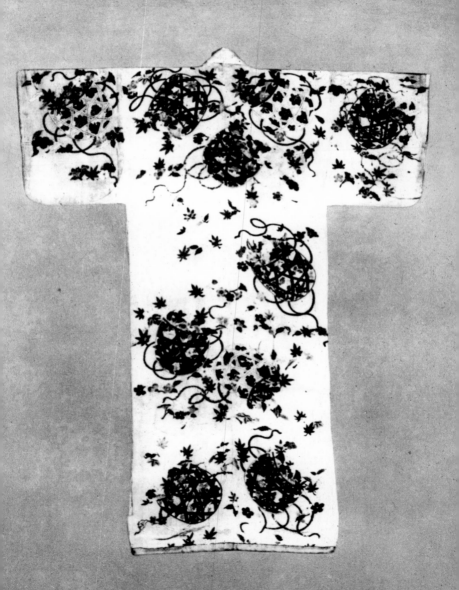

38　納戸地曳船模様小袖（部分）　江戸中期　勝川春章筆　京都　丸紅
KOSODE, YŪZEN DYEING, DESIGN BY KATSUKAWA SHUNSHŌ (detail).
Middle Edo Period. *Marubeni Collection, Kyoto.*

39　黒紅地枝垂桜鳥模様厚板唐織（能衣裳）江戸中期　東京国立博物館
NOH PLAY COSTUME, ATSUITA-KARAORI TYPE.
Middle Edo Period. *National Museum, Tokyo.*

40 & 41 赤地松竹梅君が代模様打掛　江戸中期　東京国立博物館
UCHIKAKE (lady's ceremonial gown), EMBROIDERY WITH " PINE-
BAMBOO-PLUM " DESIGN ON RED GROUND.
Middle Edo Period. *National Museum, Tokyo.*

42 赤地桜に薬玉模様打掛　江戸中期　東京国立博物館
UCHIKAKE, EMBROIDERY.
Middle Edo Period. *National Museum, Tokyo.*

43 紅葉に鷹模様小袖　江戸中期　鎌倉　長尾美術館
KOSODE, YŪZEN DYEING.
Middle Edo Period. *Nagao Museum, Kamakura.*

44 赤地松竹梅鶴亀模様振袖　江戸中期　京都　丸紅
FURISODE, TIE-DYEING (detail).
Middle Edo Period. *Marubeni Collection Kyoto.*

45　白地衝立に鷹模様小袖　江戸後期　東京　大彦染繡美術研究所
KOSODE, YŪZEN DYEING WITH EMBROIDERY (detail).
Late Edo Period. *Daihiko Institute of Dyeing and Embroidery,*
Tokyo.

46 白地草花模様打掛　江戸後期　東京国立博物館
UCHIKAKE, FLORAL DESIGN IN EMBROIDERY ON WHITE GROUND.
Late Edo Period. *National Museum, Tokyo.*

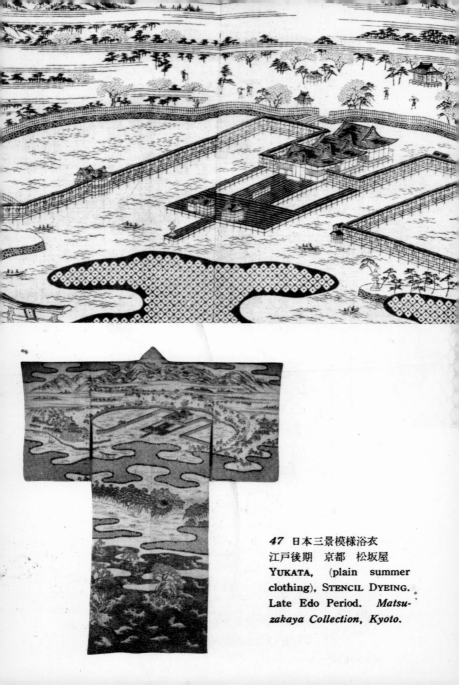

47 日本三景模様浴衣
江戸後期　京都　松坂屋
YUKATA, (plain summer clothing), STENCIL DYEING. Late Edo Period. *Matsuzakaya Collection, Kyoto.*

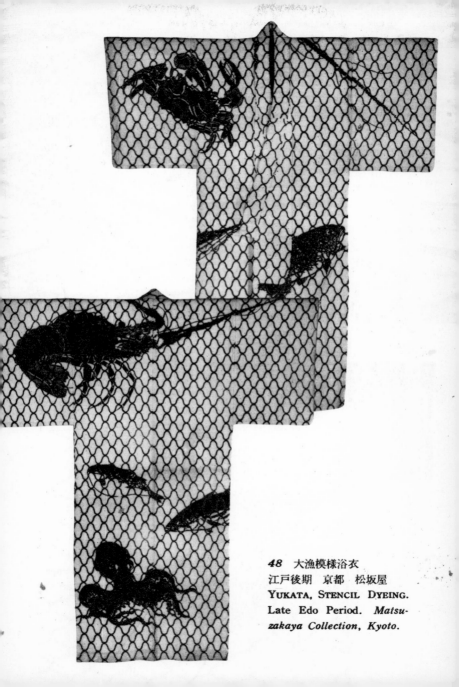

48　大漁模様浴衣
江戸後期　京都　松坂屋
YUKATA, STENCIL DYEING.
Late Edo Period. *Matsu-*
zakaya Collection, Kyoto.

49 大漁模様浴衣（部分）
Detail of Plate 48.

50　赤地違鎌模様陣羽織　桃山時代　東京国立博物館
JIMBAORI (coat worn over armour).
Momoyama Period. *National Museum, Tokyo.*

51　伏せ籠　鎌倉　長尾美術館
DRESS-SCENTING RACK. *Nagao Museum, Kamakura.*

(*continued from p. 6*)

velvets from Europe, and cottons from the South Seas. These entered Japan by way of Hakata and Sakai, the southern ports nearest the Asiatic mainland, and the new weaving techniques they inspired gradually spread to the capital at Kyoto. These new methods not only had considerable influence upon the traditional methods but continue to exert an influence today.

Momoyama-Edo period (1569–1867). The long era of peace in the Momoyama-Edo period presents a bright and splendid evolution in the history of Japanese textile art. The keynote of the age was the perfection of the Kosode (literally, "small sleeve") mode. People of all classes adopted this new style during this period, and no longer was the dyeing and weaving handicraft exclusively for the upper classes. Various artisan groups were formed to cater to the different social classes, resulting in an increased dispersion of textile art.

The prevailing characteristic of the whole period was the complete change from the small regular woven designs to designs dyed by handpainting. By the end of the Momoyama period the designs had become skillful creations of embroidery and handpainted dyed designs. The masterpieces of the time were sumptuous designs of applied gold and silver leaf and embroidery. Until the perfection of Yuzen dyeing (Plates 30 & 31) in the middle of the seventeenth century, these lavish designs and those of the tie-and-dye method were the outstanding designs in Kosode, with elegant gold brocades used in some of the outer garments. By Edo times the designs had an added picturesque freedom which culminated in the huge designs splashed across the shoulder or diagonally down the back—a design called Kambun (Plate 34).

With the perfection of the Yuzen technique (see page 64 for a description of the procedure followed in Yuzen dyeing), which produced a handpainted dyed design by using rice paste as a resist, the ultimate aim of Kosode decoration was achieved. Embroidery now came to be used as a means of enhancing and highlighting the handpainted design of the Yuzen dyeing, which was set off the better by a somewhat longer sleeve style than had been the vogue since the Kosode superseded the Junihitoe. In addition, the development of the obi or sash added a certain elegance and grace to the silhouette.

The golden age of the Kosode textiles was reached by the middle of the Edo period. By then the great emphasis on strenghtening production in each and every fief by rival daimyo had built up a flourishing textile industry in which each locality had its own speciality—hand-dyed and -woven fabrics of exceptional quality and durability, such as the famous Yuki Tsumugi silks, linens, and cottons.

As was inevitable, with the pinnacle reached not only in the dyeing and weaving handicrafts but in other forms of culture, a decadence set in; the power of designing became completely exhausted, and what had been a successful art degenerated into a mere display of technical virtuosity by skilled artisans. But again a new mode arose to create a demand for new designs and techniques, this time among the increasingly wealthy and influential merchant class, which the aristocracy attempted to keep in line by various laws and decrees against their wearing too elaborate costumes; and a noticeable feature of the time was a trend toward the *shibui* (quiet) taste of such special local weaves as Kihachijo, Yuki Tsumugi, and Echigo Chijimi in their quiet patterns of stripes, plaids, and splashes—fabrics of such good taste that they can still be worn today with an air of chic.

Meiji period (1868–1912). The Meiji period witnessed a revolution in the textile industry with the introduction of large-scale-industry methods and chemical dyeing techniques from the West, notably electric weaving looms and chemical dyes and fibers.

Although modern textiles have a new and special beauty of their own, given them by scientific progress, they have not entirely eclipsed the beauty or the popularity of hand-dyed and -woven fabrics, nor, it is to be sincerely hoped, will they ever. Surely a history of over two thousand years of a precious talent has created an instinct which will never entirely perish. This artistic feeling for design, evidenced in every period of Japanese history, is a heritage to be kept alive and developed.

Comments on the Illustrations

1. JUNIHITOE. The Chinese-style attire of the Nara period gradually changed to a native Japanese style. Shown here is the result of this evolution as perfected in the eleventh and twelfth centuries. It is a set of a noblewoman's ceremonial robes properly termed a Court Lady's Robe or a Karaginu-mo but also called a Junihitoe (12 layers of kimono). This latter appellation, however, does not mean that exactly twelve layers were worn. It is said that in the Heian period fifteen or even twenty layers of kimono were worn. Characteristic of this style was the color effect created by the several layers of kimono and the beautiful long flowing lines, although the main point was the harmony of combined colors of plain, solid-color kimonos. This illustration is of robes used in the enthronement ceremony of the late Emperor Taisho in 1915.

2. BUDDHIST PARADISE EMBROIDERY. This is the finest specimen of early Japanese embroidery for which there is authentic historical data. It is a fragment of a wall hanging which Princess Tachibana-no-Oira-tsume had embroidered after the sudden death of Crown Prince Shotoku in 621. It depicted the prince's life in Paradise and was made as a prayer for his soul's repose. It is difficult to imagine what the hanging was like in its original state as all that remains of it is a framed fragment about one meter square. Its value is mainly in the light it throws on the customs of the time and on the highly developed techniques of embroidery.

3. KANTO BROCADE. Although called a brocade, in reality this is a Kasuri weave in that it is not a design made by the weaving of several colors into the fabric, but is made by previously dyed threads used in the warp. The division of colors is very complicated and shows a very high level of weaving art. As a great number of Horyu-ji treasures were personal belongings of Crown Prince Shotoku, this is sometimes called "Crown-Prince Kanto."

4. SHU-CHIANG BROCADE. In the middle of the Meiji period most of the treasures connected with Prince Shotoku, mainly of the seventh and eighth centuries, were presented to the Imperial Household and are today preserved in the National Museum in Ueno Park, Tokyo. This *sage obi* (hanging sash) that belonged to the prince's consort is one of them. It is made of brocade in which the pattern is woven in the warp by three-color sets of threads. Two such sets were used here, one of red, yellow, and green threads, and the other of red, white and blue. Shu-chiang brocade was made in Shu-chiang Province, today known as

Szechwan, in the vicinity of Chengtu. This same kind of brocade has been excavated from graveyards in China dating back to the Han dynasty, so it can really be said to be one of the oldest kinds of brocade existing.

5. CLAMP-DYED SILK GAUZE. This is a piece of Ra dyed in the clamped-stencil technique (misprinted in the illustration caption as jammed dyeing) which flourished in the Nara period. The material was folded double, clamped between two thin boards in which the design was cut, and then dyed. The particular details of the method are unknown. Ra, the finest of the three silk gauzes—Ra, Sha, and Ro—is an exquisitely fine fabric of a very complicated weave which even today is very difficult to make. Examined closely, a small diamond-shape design appears to be woven by a twisting of the threads in the warp. This particular method of weaving is now designated as an "intangible cultural asset" by the Japanese government.

6. FLORAL-DESIGN EMBROIDERY. This beautiful floral design is embriodered on Aya silk bordered with a narrow edging of brocade. It was one of the hanging decorations of a canopy, something like the decoration around a marquee. It is very elaborate, with the embroidery executed exactly the same on both sides. The flowers and leaves are profusely embroidered in a shading of colors which was very popular during the Nara period. Color-shading was not restricted to the fabrics of the day but was widely used—even in painting Buddhist images.

7. TSUJIGAHANA DYEING. Tsujigahana dyeing, a picturesque hand-painted design combined with the well-known tie-and-dye method, was developed in the Muromachi-Momoyama period. Yuzen dyeing, a hand-painted design dyeing using a rice-paste resist, had not yet been perfected so that, other than tie-and-dye dyeing or bold embroidery designs, there were no other means of designing. The Tsujigahana designs had an inexpressibly elegant and intimate beauty that could not be found in embroidered designs.

8. NOH COSTUME. This is a Noh costume from the early Edo period and is classified as a Nuihaku or embroidered costume. The whole grey-blue ground of the kimono represents the sea on which waves are appliquéd in gold leaf and Dutch sailing ships and flowers are embroidered. The design and idea are very striking and the placing of the large and small boats and the color harmony are faultless. A really marvelous effect is created in the realistic appearance of the ships when viewed from a slant and the originality of the overflowing load of large flowers. Among the many Edo-period costumes still extant, few can compare with this in the forcefulness of the design.

9 & 10. KOSODE. The embroidered kimono illustrated here is known

as a Kosode or short-sleeved kimono. At the end of the Momoyama period and the beginning of the Edo period gold appliqué and very fine, small embroidery was in vogue. These were combined with tie-and-dye dyeing, and some very skillfully executed designs were created. In some very lavish Kosode the material was completely hidden by the gold appliqué and fine embroidery. Black, brown, or red were the colors usually used in the material. The composition of the design was large, which, contrasting with the very fine, minute embroidery, created a very effective, harmonious unity of the rich gold appliqué and exquisitely executed embroidery.

11. KOKECHI. This is a specimen of the tie-and-dye technique. Among the Shoso-in textiles some of the tie-and-dye fabrics, if scrutinized closely, reveal an exceedingly difficult technique. They are far different from those of today as they appear to have really been sewn, not merely tied. This specimen is of a very thin, flat-weave silk, probably originally red but now faded to a light brown. The delicate shading around the edge of the design well agrees with the light texture of the material.

12. BROCADE. This is a fragment of one of the most magnificent designs among the brocades preserved in the Shoso-in at Nara. Originally the piece of material of which this is a part was no doubt a bag for a *biwa*, the Japanese lute, as it is cut in the shape of that instrument. Part of it, lined with red felt, had been made into a cushion lining for some kind of box. It was not until this fragment had been discovered that the whole design of the material was revealed—and therein lies the fragment's great value. The material is Yoko brocade (pattern in the woof) in which there are many more colors and a much larger design than in Tate brocade (pattern in the warp), thus representing an advance in the technique of brocade weaving.

13. ROKECHI (BATIK). Rokechi or wax dyeing is the same as the very popular Rozome of today. In this piece the ground color is red and the leaves and flowers are in a color scheme of yellow, light brown, and red shaded from light to dark. The colors are dyed in three steps with the lightest being applied first. The design itself consists of flower-decorated canopies with hanging branches and flying birds. It has much of the feeling of serenity that distinguishes the Tempyo period (the third and final Nara art period, 725–94, considered to have been the golden age of Buddhist art in Japan) and is a design that, for that time, must have entailed considerable work.

14. YAMATO BROCADE. This is a curtain that was used around the open-air stage of Bugaku (court dancing) and is now preserved in the Kyo-o-goku-ji, a temple in Kyoto, along with other Kamakura-period musical instruments and costumes. It is a meter wide and very long, with a

ground color of green and a design of peonies and lotuses. The design and style are very conventional, having none of the scope and freedom of Nara-period designs, but the curtain is valuable because it comes from a period of which there are very few relics of Japanese dyeing and weaving.

15. TIE-DYEING. This is of interest as an example of diagonal hook-tied tie-dyeing on twill. At first glance, the design is similar to the well-known Kanoko (polka dot) tied-and-dyed design. The dots, however, are not umbrella shaped as in Kanoko and some are thick and some thin because the material was folded, hook-tied, and then dyed.

16. YAMAMOTO BROCADE. The material illustrated here is from the sash-like object which hangs from the right shoulder of a priest's robe. This particular piece belonged to the prince-priest Seishin Hoshinno (died 1085). The ground color is blue with a design of Buddhist symbolic devices. The brocaded design is of flaming scared gems on red lotuses. While there may be a lack of individuality in the stiffness of the flames, there is a definite three-dimensional quality in the design of the lotus petals. This piece of brocade is an excellent example of the better Yamato brocades of the period.

17. NOH COSTUME. The Atsuita-type Noh costume is used in por-traying male characters. Each half of the kimono is of a different material. This somewhat decadent effect is noticeable in Kamakura-period court costumes and in the dress of the Momoyama and early Edo periods. Kosode of these half-and-half designs frequently achieved stunning effects. One side of this Atsuita is of gold thread, the other of crimson satin. The designs are poetical characters from an anthology of Japanese-Chinese poetry. No two characters are the same and each is woven so skillfully that it looks like hand calligraphy.

18 & 19. NOH COSTUME. This costume dates from around the end of the Momoyama period. It is a marvelous piece of embroidery, especially the exquisite needlework of the court carriages, the stitches of which are finer than any brush could paint. The elegant court carriages and heavy-laden stems of large lilies are embroidered over the whole of the costume, with flowing vertical lines appliquéd in gold leaf in the background. The material itself is a flat-weave, brown silk. From the Momoyama period to early Edo the effect of perspective in textile designing became very popular. There are few other examples where this type of design has been handled as boldly or as effectively in a kimono as in the one illustrated here.

20 & 21. KOSODE, YUZEN DYEING. Yuzen dyeing was remarkably well developed by the middle of the Edo period. So picturesque were the designs employed in this relatively new method (tracing the outline with

a rice paste for a color resist—a process, by the way, that revolutionized the making of handpainted dyed designs) that one has the impression the kimono changed from an article of clothing to an object to be looked at. Designs were no longer limited to flowers and birds but utilized scenic and narrative themes as well. On this Kosode, probably made for the wife of a wealthy merchant, we have a scene in the Yoshiwara gay quarters of old Tokyo. In taste, this Kosode is so overly sophisticated as to be decadent, but from the point of view of execution it is a marvelous piece of workmanship.

22 & 23. NOH COSTUME. Karaori originally was the name given to all Chinese silk, "kara" meaning China. In the Heian period most brocades of gold and glossy silk threads, like damask, were called Karaori, but when used to indicate a type of Noh costume, as in the one illustrated here, the term refers to a very elegant, short-sleeved kimono worn by actors when impersonating female characters. This costume is of the middle Edo period when the Noh costumes, combining dignity and splendor, were especially beautiful.

24. KOSODE. The design of this Kosode is executed solely in the tie-and-die method and in embroidery. Diagonal stripes of embroidery on a black ground alternate with tied-and-dyed stripes of blue and black, each stripe fitting into the other with mathematical precision. When hanging, the design of this kimono seems to have a geometrical rigidity; however, when worn, the straight lines curve around the body, causing them to look softer and creating such a fascinating effect that, as a design, this is quite unique.

25. JIMBAORI. This Jimbaori, or coat worn over armor, is believed to have been a gift from Oda Nobunaga, a great lord of the sixteenth century. The rather free design is interesting because it reflects the simple, unaffected tastes of the samurai of that time. In the Momoyama period, Jimbaori decorated with bird feathers or animal fur were quite popular; there are however, very few still extant. In this one the whole top is decorated with the feathers of some fresh-water fowl, maybe duck, and in the middle of the back is a crest-like butterfly, with spread wings, made of white feathers. The black feathers arranged in rows and fastened with paper are sewn on in overlapping rows after the manner of a thatched roof. The lower part is entirely of brocade.

26. NOH COSTUME. The contrasts in this Kosode-style costume are extreme, to say the least. The ground color is half black, half crimson. On one side there is a large design of dew-laden grasses in gold-leaf appliqué over which are scattered large fans. The other side is completely embroidered in a small arabesque design of clematis. Unfortunately, the right side has been damaged and repaired so the effect of the design is greatly diminished; the tastes characteristic of the Momoyama period,

52 赤地雪持柳模様縫箔 (能衣裳) 桃山時代　岐阜　春日神社
NOH PLAY COSTUME, NUIHAKU TYPE.
Momoyama Period. *Kasuga Shrine, Gifu.*

however, are still to be seen in the gold-leaf appliqué and embroidery.

27. KOSODE.　This Kosode is believed to have been a gift from Tokugawa Ieyasu, the first of the Tokugawa shoguns, to the head of the
Sagi school of Kyogen or Noh comedy. It was a great honor for an
actor to receive garments from illustrious personages which bore the
bestower's family crest. The kimono illustrated here, presented as a
tribute to the actor's ability, bears the Tokugawa family crest in the
traditional five positions, three of which can be seen here. The upper
shoulder part is dyed purple in a double-diamond shape. On one side
there is a large bamboo stalk dyed green by the tie-and-dye method.
From this stalk branch out new shoots in pale blue-green. Aside from

53 亀甲模様縫箔打掛（北政所所用）桃山時代　京都　高台寺
UCHIKAKE NUIHAKU, TYPE.
Momoyama Period. *Kō-daiji Temple, Kyoto.*

the fine hand-outlining of the edges of the leaves and stalk in India ink, the whole kimono is dyed in the tie-and-dye method of the early Edo period.

28. FURISODE. This long-sleeved kimono belonged to Keishonin, the mother of the fifth Tokugawa shogun, Tsunayoshi, and has been preserved among the treasures of the Gokoku-ji, a temple in Tokyo, which, incidentally, was built on the order of Keishonin. The design's distinguishing feature is a large plum tree with spreading branches in stencil-dyeing separating the black ground and the polka-dot design. The design is indicative of the coming style in huge designs of the Kambun-Genroku period.

29. KOSODE. This exquisite design by the great painter and founder of the Korin school, Ogata Korin, reveals his genius despite its having been executed within the restricting confines of a kimono. This Kosode was painted for the wife of a rich Edo merchant named Fuyuki and so is called the Fuyuki Kosode. The material is white satin, on which are painted clumps of autumnal grasses which range from black to the lightest colors. The clumps, painted with free brush strokes, are cleverly arranged so that the effect of the painting is best shown when it is worn.

30 & 31. KOSODE. The development of Yuzen dyeing in the middle Edo period provided the means of making the Kosode unbelievably beautiful. Embroidery, which had played a leading role in enhancing hand-dyed designs before the time of Yuzen dyeing, now no longer needed to be used to give depth to the designs. In this Kosode the upper part has variously shaped designs scattered over a crimson background. The lower part is a superb landscape dyed in many colors on a white background. This garment is an excellent example of how much colorful beauty the Yuzen method added to the kimono, especially as by this time the obi had been recognized as a necessary complement to the costume.

32 & 33. NOH COSTUME. The name Atsuita Karaori is used for especially beautiful Noh costumes used when portraying male characters. The robe shown here reveals the refined dignity of a design typical of this kind of costume. The background is a checkerboard pattern in gold on a light-blue ground. Clematis, in an arabesque design woven in many colors, cover the whole kimono. The pale-blue background and beautiful flowers effectively balance any appearance of heaviness resulting from the lavish use of gold.

34. KOSODE. The Kambun design on this Kosode is a typical example of the huge shoulder design that suddenly became popular in the Kambun era (1661–73). The material of this garment is white silk-damask while the huge chrysanthemums which form part of the design are made by the tie-and dye process. A design like this is especially attractive on a kimono tied with a narrow obi.

35. FURISODE. In the execution of this boldly designed kimono, practically every technique in use in the Edo period has been employed—Yuzen dyeing, tie-and-dye, gold-leaf appliqué, and embroidery. In imagination and individuality it is most typical of that colorful period. The material is crimson silk-damask. A huge design of a sheaf of *noshi* (a ceremonial decoration used on gift packages) splashed completely across the back makes this truly spectacular Kosode representative of the ultimate beauty achieved in designing and dyeing.

36. KOSHIMAKI. Koshimaki is the name of a ceremonial summer robe worn by court ladies at the palace in Edo times. A hemp kimono tied

with a narrow sash was worn underneath and the Koshimaki was merely wrapped around the body. The material was always black or dark brown and the lining crimson. The auspicious design of turtle, crane, and *sho-chiku-bai* (plum, bamboo, and pine) are beautifully embroidered over the whole of this one. The turtle and crane are symbols of longevity while the *sho-chiku-bai* symbolizes strength, uprightness, and fidelity. Among the extant women's kimonos of the Edo period this probably is one that has entailed the greatest labor.

37. Kosode. Designs which incorporate only Yuzen dyeing are often rather garish looking. This garish effect was avoided in the illustrated Kosode by combining Yuzen dyeing with embroidery to create this charming design. Large flower baskets of many shaded colors, stuffed with flowers and maple leaves, are cleverly placed on a blue background so pale it appears white. Some flowers and leaves are effectively scattered about outside of the baskets as though they were being scattered by a breeze.

38. Koshimaki. As Yuzen dyeing steadily progressed, the designs became increasingly picturesque. Frequently, noted painters of the day adapted their creations to the confines of the dyeing technique. The design shown in this illustration is by the Ukiyo-e painter Katsukawa Shinsho. Although it is not in his field of genre painting, the design is valued as an original work of a noted artist. White waves are embroidered around the realistically sketched towboat on a background of dark blue. The effect of the kimono as a whole is very pleasing.

39. Noh Costume. The skillful weaving of this costume is incredibly beautiful. The design, consisting of birds woven in dazzling colors of red, green, purple, and yellow, flying through the hanging boughs of a weeping cherry tree, stands out brilliantly on the elegant, deep-black background.

40 & 41. Uchikake. The ceremonial outer garment of court ladies in the Edo period was called an Uchikake or sometimes Kaidori. It differed from the Kosode in that no obi was used and the back was completely covered with a very large, attractive design. The proper colors for such robes were red, white, or black. The design of this robe consists of the symbolic pine-bamboo-plum motif and the embroidered characters of *Kimigayo,* the national anthem. Although the calligraphy adds a bit of stiffness, there is much charm in this auspicious design. The garment appears to have originally been a Furisode, later converted into a Uchikake by shortening the sleeves.

42. Uchikake. As Uchikake were not worn with an obi one might reasonably conclude that their designs would have much freedom. In that they are ceremonial court costumes however, they are more ornate

54 赤地吉祥模様袱紗　江戸中期　奈良　興福院
FUKUSA (gift cover), EMBROIDERY.
Middle Edo Period. *Kombuin Temple, Nara.*

than the Kosode and have rather stiff and standardized designs. This is
a red Uchikake with a refined design of cherry blossoms and palace
appurtenances—bamboo curtains of state and beautifully decorated,
hanging scent balls. The graceful design is very deftly handled with
a balanced use of tie-and-dye and embroidery.

43. KOSODE. This Kosode design is an attempt to achieve the half-and-half effect so much the vogue from the Momoyama to early Edo period by a horizontal division in place of the more common vertical division. The upper half is a geometrical check design of black and white with large crest of calligraphy characters on the back and sleeves. Contrasting with this, the Yuzen-dyed design on the lower half is of maple, bamboo, and phoenix in many colors. This lower design, although similar to the scroll paintings of the famous Kano school, seems a bit overdone, thus weakening the forceful effect of the upper half. Even so, it is a superb costume.

44. FURISODE. The tie-and-die method, practiced in Japan from early times, reached its highest stage of perfection after the middle of the Edo period. On this kimono can be seen the skilled throwing-in-relief of the design on a background done entirely in the tie-and-dye method. The design consists of the symbolic motif of turtle, crane, and *sho-chiku-bai*. The amount of labor that must have been required to produce such a piece of tied-and-dyed material is hardly conceivable in the present day.

45. KOSODE. The Yuzen-dyeing technique also reached its highest peak of success in the later Edo period. The most popular designs were in the Kaga Yuzen style of dyeing in gradations of shaded colors. Aside from the blue of the screen the whole design is really a fine example of the use of color in Yuzen dyeing. It is so well executed that all of the tracing outlines are in perfect alignment at the seams. The plum blossoms on the screen and the fettered hawk on top of it are done in embroidery and are, as is the whole Kosode, the products of masterly workmanship.

46. UCHIKAKE. This Uchikake was worn by a mistress of the thirteenth Tokugawa shogun, Iesada. As might be expected in a costume of a shogun's mistress, it has a high degree of refinement, showing none of the decadence that was conspicuous in the designs of the later Edo period. This kimono was made of white silk-damask with flowing diagonal designs and flowers of the various seasons.

47. YUKATA. The Yukata is a kimono worn after bathing—a cool, comfortable garment for summer. Clear-cut designs in dark blue were most popular, some of them being of very complicated designs for which dozens of stencils were required. On this one is a design depicting three famous landscapes: Miyajima, Hashidate, and Matsushima. It is typical of the taste of the merchants of this time.

48 & 49. YUKATA. On this Yukata the whole design is of a fish net, with lobsters, octopus, crab, and globefish caught here and there in the net. As a design it is bold and has a humorous keynote. When examined at firsthand, the face of the globefish actually has an expression of

55 かきつばた模様縫箔 江戸後期 東京国立博物館
NOH PLAY CUSTUME, NUIHAKU TYPE.
Late Edo Period. *National Museum, Tokyo.*

surprise that, regretably, cannot be seen in this illustration. Although the design on this Yukata appears to be rather simple, it really required an extravagant number of stencils.

50. JIMBAORI. This coat is believed to have belonged to Kobayakawa Hideaki, a samurai of the Momoyama period. It is made of red woolen cloth and is only faintly kimono-like in design, having probably been copied from Dutch garments of the time. The bold design of crossed sickles in appliqué of black and white woolen material agrees favorably with the shape of the coat. Woolen materials were all imported at this time.

51. DRESS-SCENTING RACK. This rack is made of lacquered rods tied together in such a way as to allow it to be folded up when not in use. Garments were placed over this rack and scented by burning incense beneath them.

52. NOH COSTUME. From ancient times religious Noh dances or Kagura have been performed at the Kasuga Shrine in Gifu Prefecture, at which are preserved a number of sets of costumes and masks. All of the costumes are of the pre-Momoyama period and most of them are embroidered. This one is of a red material with snow-covered willows and tied-and-dyed butterflies in large rings. The excellent designing of the young willow, with snow-laden leaves of green and yellow covering the whole kimono, is most effective.

53. UCHIKAKE. This ceremonial robe belonged to Kita-no-Mandokoro, wife of Toyotomi Hideyoshi, military ruler from 1582 to 1598. It is preserved in the Kodai-ji (a temple in Kyoto built by order of Kita-no-Mandokoro) along with many other authentic belongings of Hideyoshi and his wife. The whole of the garment is covered with embroidered tortoise-shell patterns with diamond-shaped conventionalized flower designs in each tortoise shell. The color harmony of light green, purple, and blue, the silver appliqué, and the exquisite needlework of the embroidery make it one of the finest examples of Japanese workmanship as well as a piece of handiwork that adds luster to the Momoyama age.

54. FUKUSA. This gift-cover is preserved in the Kombu-in, a convent in Nara. In 1713 Abbotess Amagimi of this convent came to Edo and was received in audience by Lady Zuishonin, the wife of the fourth Tokugawa shogun, Ietsuna. She received as a gift from Lady Zuishonin a cloth cover of nine pieces sewn together. The cover has been separated into thirty-one pieces, of which this gift-cover is one.

55. NOH COSTUME. This costume is of satin material in which the warp threads were dyed in even lengths of white, red, purple, and light green. The whole kimono has a basket-weave appliqué of gold leaf with clumps of irises embroidered in several colors at the bottom and across the top. It is a dazzling thing with its shining satin, gold, and brilliant colors.

56. PENDANT ORNAMENT. This is a hanging decoration for a type of festival cart which was widely in use during the later Edo period. The material is red wool with a very richly embroidered white tiger on the back and on the front an imaginary animal known as a *raiju*. The feeling of strength in the pose of the tiger makes it a splendid-looking hanging for a festival cart. The embroidery of the late Edo period attained an exceedingly high level, but in some aspects became rather

56 山車の飾幕　江戸後期　個人所有
PENDENT ORNAMENT FOR FESTIVAL CART.
Late Edo Period. *Private Collection.*

garish. It was very heavily padded—dazzling sometimes, with gold and glass embroidered into the designs; however, depending on the use, such designs could be very effective, as in the case of this hanging decoration.

57 & 58. MODELS WEARING FURISODE AND KOSODE. Pictured here is the contrast between the long-sleeved Furisode and the short-sleeved Kosode. On the latter can be seen the effect of the continuity of the design. This placing of the design on what is practically one piece of material (the kimono has no shoulder seam) so as to retain the continuity of design at the sleeve seams and side seams is an important device in designing handed down from the Momoyama period.

57. 江戸中期頃の御殿女中の振袖姿
MODEL. COURT ATTENDANT
IN FURISODE.　Late Edo Period.

58.　元禄頃の小袖
MODEL. WOMAN IN KOSODE.
Genroku (Early Edo) Period.

APPLYING COLOR

Yuzen Dyeing

The method of Yuzen dyeing practiced today is, aside from the fact that chemical dyes are used, exactly the same as it was when first developed in the seventeenth century. The discovery that the juice of the *tsuyukusa* flower (the common commelina or *commelina communis*) could be easily rinsed off the material, after being applied to trace the design, resulted in a dyeing technique that revolutionized the handicraft of handpainted-dyed designing, and made possible the breath-takingly beautiful results we can see today.

METHOD IN BRIEF: The juice extracted from the tsuyukusa flower is applied in a fine line to delineate the design. This line is then retraced with a color resist made of a rice paste, usually applied with a paper funnel; occasionally, however, the old method of using a chopstick-like instrument is employed. The outlined design is then filled in with the desired color or colors, steamed to set the color, and then covered with the resist and dried.

64

MODERN METHOD OF APPLYING RESIST.

Next the whole background is painted in, steamed, and dried. The material is then immersed in fast-running water, ideally a stream, until the rice-paste resist and tracing fluid are removed—a process which takes about ten minutes.

The final steps are to dry the material, steam it to remove wrinkles, and finally stretch it to an even width.

OLD METHOD OF APPLYING RESIST.

茜草（あかね）

紅花（べにばな）

蘇芳（すおう）

紫根（しこん）

藍（あい）

欝金（うこん）

黄蘗（きはだ）

Color No. 1. *Madder*. Perennial vine with long, egg-shaped, thorny leaves. Roots of three-year-old plant used for dye.

Color No. 2. *Safflower* (Chrysanthemum family). Perennial. The flowers are reddish-yellow. Plant looks like a wild thistle and grows to a height of one meter. Flowers used for dye.

Color No. 3. *Judas tree*. The bark of this deciduous plant is used as a medicine as well as for making dye. Its yellow flowers are used in making a red paint used by artists.

Color No. 4. *Shikon*. A perennial plant with five-petal flowers. The dark purple skin of its thick roots is used for dye.

Color No. 5. *Ai* (Indigo plant). Annual. Brought to Japan from French Indo-China in ancient times. Its red flowers bloom in autumn. Leaves used for dye.

Color No. 6. *Turmeric*. Perennial member of the ginger family. Its tuber roots are dried and used for dye.

Color No. 7. *Kihada*. A deciduous tree. Its bark is used for medicine and dye.

Color No. 8. *Rhubarb.* Perennial. The Japanese variety has a whitish-yellow flower. Roots are used for dye.

大<ruby>だ<rt></rt></ruby>黄<ruby>おう<rt></rt></ruby>

Color No. 9. *Gardenia.* Evergreen. The ripe yellow seeds are used for making dye.

支<ruby>くち<rt></rt></ruby>子<ruby>なし<rt></rt></ruby>

Color No. 10. *Kariyasu.* A perennial plant that resembles pampas grass. Leaves and stems used for dye.

刈<ruby>かり<rt></rt></ruby>安<ruby>やす<rt></rt></ruby>

Color No. 11. *Mochi Tsutsuji* (a variety of azalea). The leaves of this evergreen bush are used for dye.

黐<ruby>もち<rt></rt></ruby>躑<ruby>つつ<rt></rt></ruby>躅<ruby>じ<rt></rt></ruby>

Color No. 12. *Yashabushi* (member of birch family.) The seeds of this deciduous tree are used for dye.

やしゃぶし

Color No. 13. *Alder.* Deciduous tree. The bark of this tree is used for dye.

榛<ruby>はんのき<rt></rt></ruby>

Color No. 14. *Sumac.* Deciduous. Was used in ancient times for making wax. Dye is made from its bark.

櫨<ruby>はじ<rt></rt></ruby>

Color No. 15. *Pomegranate.* The fruit of this deciduous tree is used for dye.

石<ruby>ざく<rt></rt></ruby>榴<ruby>ろ<rt></rt></ruby>

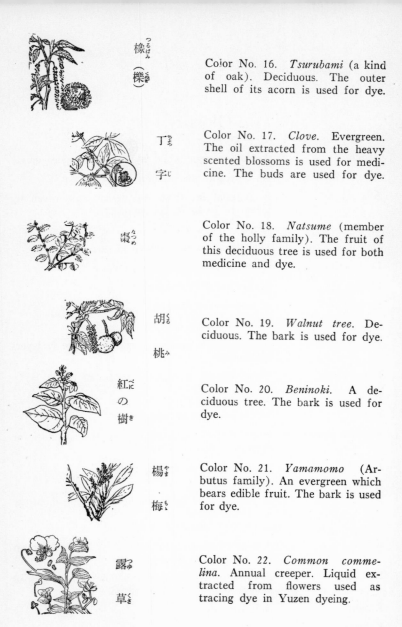

橡 つるばみ
（櫟）くぬぎ

Color No. 16. *Tsurubami* (a kind of oak). Deciduous. The outer shell of its acorn is used for dye.

丁 ちょう
字 じ

Color No. 17. *Clove.* Evergreen. The oil extracted from the heavy scented blossoms is used for medicine. The buds are used for dye.

棗 なつめ

Color No. 18. *Natsume* (member of the holly family). The fruit of this deciduous tree is used for both medicine and dye.

胡 くる
桃 み

Color No. 19. *Walnut tree.* Deciduous. The bark is used for dye.

紅 べに
の
樹 き

Color No. 20. *Beninoki.* A deciduous tree. The bark is used for dye.

楊 やま
梅 もも

Color No. 21. *Yamamomo* (Arbutus family). An evergreen which bears edible fruit. The bark is used for dye.

露 つゆ
草 くさ

Color No. 22. *Common commelina.* Annual creeper. Liquid extracted from flowers used as tracing dye in Yuzen dyeing.

Glossary

Atsuita	A Noh costume worn in portraying male roles
Atsuita Karaori	An especially fine Atsuita Noh Costume
Aya	A material in which the design was woven by means of twills or plaited weaves
Chirimen	Crepe
Donsu	Silk damask with a design in satin
Echigo Chijimi	A hemp crepe of Echigo Province
Fukusa	A traditional cloth cover for gifts
Furisode	A long-sleeved kimono
Jimbaori	A garment worn over armor
Junihitoe	A court-lady's costume consisting of many layers of kimono
Kaga Yuzen	Yuzen dyeing in gradated shades of colors
Kaiki	Taffeta
Kame	Turtle—symbol of longevity
Kambun designs	Huge designs splashed across the shoulder or diagonally down the back
Kanto Brocade	Flat-woof weave of mottled threads
Karaori	1. Chinese silk 2. Brocades of gold and glossy silk threads of the Heian period 3. A very elegant Noh costume
Kasuri	A splashed design made by pre-dyed threads woven in silk or cotton materials
Kihachijo	A thin, soft, plain-woven yellow silk in striped designs made on Hachijo Island
Kinran	Gold brocade
Kokechi	*See* Shibori

Koshimaki	A court-lady's ceremonial summer garment
Kosode	A short-sleeved kimono
Kyokechi	Stencil dyeing
Nishiki	Brocade
Nuihaku	Embroidery and gold-leaf appliqué
Obi	Sash
Ojiya Chijimi	A hemp crepe, from the vicinity of Ojiya, in Kasuri or striped designs
Omeshi	A flat silk crepe in Kasuri or striped or plaid designs
Oshima	A flat silk in Kasuri design originally made on Oshima Island
Rinzu	Silk damask with geometrical woven designs
Ra	Silk gauze of a stiff textured open weave
Ro	Silk gauze with vertical or horizontal stripes of open weave
Rokechi	Batik dyeing
Sha	Silk gauze of soft textured open weave
Shibori	Tie-and-dye method of hand dyeing
Sho-chiku-bai	Auspicious design of pine, bamboo, and plum— symbols of fidelity, uprightness, and strength, respectively
Tate Nishiki	Brocade with the pattern in the warp
Tsujigahana dyeing	A combination of Shibori dyeing and hand-painted designs
Tsuru	Crane—symbol of longevity and luck
Tsuzure	Linked-weave brocade or ancient silk tapestry
Uchikake	A court-lady's ceremonial outer garment
Yamato brocade	A Nara-period brocade with the design in the woof
Yoko Nishiki	A brocade with the pattern in the woof
Yukata	An informal summer kimono
Yuki Tsumugi	A rather rough weave of silk; much like a tussar weave
Yuzen dyeing	See pp. 64–65